TEXTIONARY

The Texting Dictionary

TEXTIONARY

The Texting Dictionary

By CL Hogan

Mill City Publishing
Minneapolis MN

Mill City Press, Inc.
212 3rd Avenue North, Suite 290
Minneapolis, MN 55401 612.455.2294
www.millcitypublishing.com

Textionary is compilation of popular texting acronyms, jargon and abbreviations
as well as original terms. All illustrations are royalty-free images posted on public
websites, available to download for personal use and reproduction.

ISBN - 978-1-936107-87-2
ISBN - 1-936107-87-2
LCCN – 2010927227

Printed in the United States of America

Thank God for using me as the vessel to put this wonderful idea into print. Special thanks to my mother for all that she endured, to my husband for sharing the dream, being my partner and all his hard work, to my daughter for her 2 cents and to my family for believing in me and for their input.

Why accept the ordinary, when you can have the extraordinary...

Dreams do come true...if you believe

THE TEXTING DICTIONARY

INVENTORY OF INTERNET ACRONYMS & WORDING COMMUNICATION TERMINOLOGY

Generally used anywhere individuals go online – as seen in IM, text messages, email, SMS, cell phone, Blackberry, iPhone, , PDA, handy or pager -- and as looked at on blogs, chat rooms, Web sites, games, and newsgroup postings -- these short forms are utilized by individuals to communicate with each other. Acronyms are an essential component of computer customs. The use of acronyms developed quickly on the Internet and produced a new vernacular, known as shorthand and online jargon.

Acronyms are often typed in CAPS lock although it is not appropriate netiquette to type in CAPS lock in general, in fact, it is like **SHOUTING**. People with imperfect eyesight might use all caps to distinguish the words better, but otherwise, TURN THE CAPS LOCK OFF.

Note: "C" and "S" are interchangeable for "See"; "Y", likewise, "U" and "Y" are used for "You" .

The current web vernacular is the wave of the future as commonly used acronyms have made their way into everyday conversation. Soon this may be an alternative to traditional language as its popularity steadily increases.

Textionary is a must have guide for individuals who want to decipher the lingo and slang utilized on the World Wide Web and OTW (over the wire) convos.

-NUMBERS & SYMBOLS-

!-	I have a comment
*$-	Starbucks
,!!!!-	Talk to the hand
02-	My (or your) two cents worth
10Q-	Thank you
10X-	Thanks
1174-	Nude club
121-	One to one (private chat invitation)
1337-	Leet meaning "elite"
143-	I love you
14AA41-	One for all, and all for one
182-	I hate you
187-	Homicide
19-	Zero hand (online gaming)
190-	Hand
1CE-	Once
1DR-	I wonder
2-	To
20-	Location
24/7-	24 hours a day, 7 days a week
2A2BD-	Too anointed to be disappointed
2B2BS-	Too blessed to be stressed
2B or not 2B-	To be or not to be
2B@-	To be at
2BZ4UQT-	Too busy for you cutie
2EZ-	Too easy
2G2B4G-	Too good to be forgotten

2G2BT-	Too good to be true
2H2H-	Too hot too handle
2MI-	Too much information
2M2H-	Too much too handle
2MORO-	Tomorrow
2MOR-	Tomorrow
2NITE/2NTE-	Tonight
2U2-	To you too
3HAAC-	3 hots and a cot (jail)
4-	For
404-	I haven't a clue
411-	Information
420-	Marijuana or let's get high
459-	I love you (ILY)
4COL-	For crying out loud
4EAE-	Forever and ever
4EVA-	Forever
4EVER-	Forever
4NR-	Foreigner
4Q-	Freak you
^5-	High-five
511-	Too much information
555-	Sobbing, crying (Mandarin/Chinese txt)
55555-	Crying your eyes out (Mandarin/Chinese)
55555-	Laughing (Thai- means "ha")
5FS-	5 finger salute
5STAR-	Dime, hottie, hot girl, 10, 5 star hotels, the best
6Y-	Sexy
7K-	Sick
7:30-	Not wrapped too tight, mental
8-	Oral sex
831-	I love you (8 letters, 3 words, 1 meaning)
86-	Out of, over, to get rid of, or kicked out

88-	Hugs and kisses
88-	Bye-bye (Mandarin Chinese txt)
9-	Parent is watching
99-	Parent is no longer watching
911-	Urgent, Emergency
::poof::-	I'm gone
^^-	Read line or message above
<3-	heart (sideways heart- love, friendship)
</3-	Broken heart
<33-	bigger heart or more love (more 3's mean bigger)
?-	I have a question
?-	I don't understand
?^-	hook up?
?4U-	Question for you
@TEOTD-	At the end of the day
<s>-	Smile
s-	Smile
w-	Wink
\M/-	Heavy Metal Music
^RUP^-	Read Up Please
^URS-	Up Yours

A/S/L/P-	Age/Sex/Location/Picture
A3-	Anyplace, Anywhere, Anytime
AA-	As above
AAAAA-	American Association against Acronym Abuse
AAF-	As a friend or "always and forever"
AAK-	Asleep at keyboard / alive and kicking
AAMOF-	As a matter of fact
AAMOI-	As a matter of interest
AAP-	Always a pleasure
AAR-	At any rate
AAR8-	At any rate
AAS-	Alive and smiling
AASHTA-	As always Sheldon has the answer (Bike mechanic Sheldon Brown)
AATK-	Always at the keyboard
AAYF-	As always, your friend
AB-	*Butt* backwards
AB/ABT-	About
ABC-	Already been chewed
ABITHIWTITB-	A bird in the hand is worth two in the bush
ABT2-	About To
ABTA-	Goodbye, (signoff)
ACCT#-	Account Number
ACD-	Alt/ Control /Delete
ACDNT-	Accident
ACE-	Access /Control /Entry
ACK-	Acknowledgement
ACORN-	A completely obsessive really nutty person
ACPT-	Accept

ACQSTN-	Acquisition (email, government)
ADAD-	Another day another dollar
ADBB-	All done, bye-bye
ADCT-	A dream come true
ADD-	Address
ADDY-	Address
ADIDAS-	All day I dream about sex
ADIH-	Another day in hell
ADIP-	Another day in paradise
ADMIN-	Administrator
ADMINR-	Administrator (government)
ADN-	Advanced Digital Network or any day now
ADR-	Address
ADVD-	Advised
AE-	Area effect (online gambling)
AEAP-	As early as possible
AF-	April fools
AFAGAYA-	A friend as good as you
AFAHMASP-	A fool and his money are soon parted
AFAIAA-	As far as I am aware
AFAIC-	As far as I'm concerned
AFAICS-	As far as I can see
AFAICT-	As far as I can tell
AFAIK-	As far as I know
AFAIR-	As far as I remember
AFAIU-	As far as I understand
AFAIUI-	As far as I understand it
AFAP-	As far as possible
AFAYC-	As far as you're concerned
AFC-	Away from computer
AFDN-	Any *freaking* day now
AFGO-	Another *freaking* growth opportunity
AFIAA-	As far as I am aware

AFINIAFI-	A friend in need is a friend indeed
AFJ-	April fool's joke
AFK-	Away from keyboard or a free kill
AFPOE-	A fresh pair of eyes
AFT-	About freaking time
AFZ-	Acronym free zone
AGB-	Almost good bridge
AGKWE-	And God knows what else
AH-	At home
AIAMU-	And I'm a monkey's uncle
AIGHT-	All right
AIH-	As it happens
AIMB-	As I mentioned before
AIMP-	Always In my prayers
AIR-	As I remember
AISB-	As I said before/ as it should be
AISE-	As I said earlier
AISI-	As I see it
AITR-	Adult in the room
AKA or A.K.A.-	Also known as
ALAP-	As late as possible
ALCON-	All concerned
ALOL-	Actually laughing out loud
ALOTBSOL-	Always look on the bright side of life
ALTG-	Act locally, think globally
AMAP-	As many as possible/ as much as possible
AMBW-	All my best wishes
AMF-	Adios mother *fouler*
AML-	All my love
AMOF-	A matter of fact
AMRMTYFTS-	All my roommates thank you for the show
ANFAWFOS-	And now for a word from our sponsor
ANFSCD-	And now for something completely different

ANGB-	Almost nearly good bridge
AO-	Anarchy online (online gambling)
AOAS-	All of a sudden
AOB-	Abuse of bandwidth
AOE-	Area of effect (online gambling)
AOM-	Age of majority (mythology- online gaming)
AOTA-	All of the above
AOYP-	Angel on your pillow
AON-	All or nothing
AP-	Apple Pie
APAC-	All praise and credit
APB-	All points bulletin
AQAP-	As quickly as possible
AQAQAP-	As quickly and quietly as possible
ARE-	Acronym rich environment
AS-	Ape *dodo* or another subject
ASAFP-	As soon as *freaking* possible
ASAMOF-	As a matter of fact
ASAP-	As soon as possible
ASAYGT-	As soon as you get this
ASIG-	And so it goes
ASL-	Age/sex/location
ASLA-	Age/sex/location/availability
ASLMH-	Age/sex/location/music/hobbies
AT-	At terminal
ATAB-	Ain't that a *biscuit*
ATAI-	And the answer is
ATB-	All the best
ATEOTD-	At the end of the day
ATC-	Any two cards (online gambling)
ATM-	At the moment /Automated Teller Machine/ Asynchronous Transfer Mode
ATSITS-	All the stars in the sky

ATSL-	Along the same line
ATST-	At the same time
ATW-	All the web /around the web or all the way
ATWD-	Agree that we disagree
AWC-	After while, crocodile
AWDY-	Are we done yet?
AWESO-	Awesome
AWGTHTGTTA-	Are we going to have to go through this again?
AWHFY-	Are we having fun yet?
AWLTP-	Avoiding work like the plague
AWNIAC-	All we need is another chair
AWOL-	Absent without leave
AWOL-	Away without leaving (online gaming)
AWTTW-	A word to the wise
AWTY-	Are we there yet?
AYC-	Aren't you clever / aren't you cheeky/ At your convenience
AYCE-	All you can eat
AYDY-	Are you done yet?
AYEC-	At your earliest convenience
AYK-	As you know
AYOR-	At your own risk
AYS-	Are you serious?
AYSOS-	Are you stupid or something
AYT-	Are you there?
AYTMTB-	And you're telling me this because
AYV-	Are you vertical?
AZN-	Asian

- B -

B-	Be or back
B^-	Bees up
B&-	Banned
B&F-	Back and forth
B/C-	Because
B@U-	Back at you
B2W-	Back to work
B2BW-	Born to be wild
B4-	Before
B4N-	Bye for now
B4U-	Before you
B4YKI-	Before you know it
B8-	Bait (person teased or joked with, or under-aged person/teen)
B9-	Boss is watching
BA-	Bad *butt*
BAC-	Bad *butt chick
BAG-	Busting a gut or big *butt* grin
BAHF-	Blessed and highly favored
BAK-	Back at keyboard
BAMF-	Bad butt mother *fouler*
BANANA-	Code word for penis
BARB-	Buy abroad but rent in Britain
BAS-	Big *butt* smile
BASOR-	Breathing a sigh of relief
BAU-	Business as usual
BAY-	Back at ya (you)
BB-	Be back
BB4N-	Bye-bye for now

BBAMFIC-	Big bad butt mother *fouler *in charge
BBB-	Bye-bye babe/ boring beyond belief
BBBG-	Bye-bye, be good
BBC-	Big bad challenge
BBFBBM-	Body by Fisher, brains by Mattel
BBFN-	Bye-bye for now
BBIAB-	Be back in a bit
BBIAF-	Be back in a few
BBIAM-	Be back in a minute
BBIAS-	Be back in a sec
BBIAW-	Be back in a while
BBL-	Be back later
BBMFIC-	Big bad mother *fouler* in charge
BBN-	Bye-bye now
BBR-	Burnt beyond repair
BBS-	Be back soon /bulletin board service
BBQ-	Barbeque/ shooting score online gambling
BBS-	Be back soon
BBSD-	Be back soon darling
BBSL-	Be back sooner or later
BBT-	Be back tomorrow
BBW-	Big beautiful woman
BC-	Because/ be cool
BCBG-	Bon Chic Bon Genre / Belle Cu Belle Geulle
BCBS-	Big company, big school
BCNU-	Be seeing you
BCOZ-	Because
BD-	Big Deal / Baby Dance /Brain Drain
B-DAY/BDAY-	Birthday
BDBI5M-	Busy daydreaming back in 5 minutes
BDC-	Big dumb company / big dot com

BDN-	Big darn number
BEG-	Big evil grin
BEOS-	Nudge
B/F-	Boyfriend
BF-	Best friend
BFAW-	Best friend at work
BF2-	Battlefield 2 (online gaming)
BFD-	Big *freaking* deal
BFE-	Bum *freaking* Egypt
BFF-	Best friends forever
BFFL-	Best friend for life
BFFLNMW-	Best friends for life no matter what
BFFN-	Best friends for now
BFFTTE-	Best friends forever til the end
BFG-	Big *freaking* grin
BFN-	Bye for now
BFR-	Big *freaking* rock/ be for real
BG-	Be good/ big grin
BGWM-	Be gentle with me
BG2M-	Be good to me/ been good to me
BHAG-	Big hairy audacious goal
BHG-	Big hearted guy /big hearted girl
BHIMBGO-	Bloody *Hades*, I must be getting old
BHL8-	Be home late
BHOF-	Bald headed old fart
BI-	Business intelligence/ basic intelligence
BI5-	Back in five
BIB-	Boss is back
BIBI-	Bye-bye
BIBO-	Beer in, beer out/ basic in/basic out
BIF-	Basis in fact / before I forget
BIH-	Burn in *Hades*

BIL-	Brother-in-law / boss is listening
BIO-	Bring it on
BIOIYA-	Break it off in your *butt*
BION-	Believe it or not
BIOYE-	Blow it out your ear
BIOYIOP-	Blow it out your I/O port
BIOYN-	Blow it out your nose
BI***-	Basically in the clear homey
BISFLAM-	Boy, I sure feel like a monkey
BITD-	Back in the day
BITFOB-	Bring it the *freak* on, *biscuit*
BITMT-	But in the meantime
BJ-	Blow job
BKA-	Better known as
BL-	Belly laughing
BLBBLB-	Back like bull, brain like bird
BLKBRY-	Blackberry
BLNT-	Better luck next time
BM-	Bite me/ baby mama
BMD-	Baby mama drama
BME-	Based on my experience
BMF-	Bad mother *fouler*
BMGWL-	Busting my gut with laughter
BMOC-	Big man on campus
BMOF-	Bite me old fart
BMOTA-	Bite me on the *butt*
BMS-	By myself
BMW-	Black man's woman/beautifully maintained Woman/ black man working
BM&Y-	Between me and you
BNDN-	Been nowhere done nothing
BNF-	Big name fan

BO-	Bug off / body odor
BOB-	Battery operated boyfriend/ back off buddy
BOBFOC-	Body off Baywatch, face off crime watch
BOE-	Bind on equipment (online gaming)
BOCTAAE-	But Of Course There Are Always Exceptions
BOFH-	Bastard operator from *Hades*
BOHICA-	Bend over here it comes again
BOL-	Best of luck
BOLO-	Be on the look out
BON-	Believe it or not
BOOK-	Cool
BOOMS-	Bored out of my skull
BOP-	Bind on pickup (online gaming)
BOSMKL-	Bending over smacking my knee laughing
BOT-	Back on topic/ be on that
BOTEC-	Back of the envelope calculation
BOTOH-	But on the other hand
BOYF-	Boyfriend
BPLM-	Big person little mind
BR-	Bathroom/bedroom /be real
BRB-	Be right back
BRBB-	Be right back babe
BRBNC-	Be right back, nature calls
BRD-	Bored
BRH-	Be right here
BRIC-	Brazil, Russia, India, China
BRT-	Be right there
BS-	Big smile / bull *crap*/ brain strain
BSAAW-	Big smile and a wink
BSBD&NE-	Book smart, brain dead & no experience
BSEG-	Big *dodo* eating grin
BSF-	But seriously, folks
BSOD-	Blue screen of death

BSTS-	Better safe than sorry
BT-	Bite this/ between technologies
BTA-	But then again / before the attacks
BTD-	Bored to death
BTDT-	Been there, done that
BTDTGTS-	Been there, done that, got the t-shirt
BTFO-	Back the *freak* off / bend the *freak* over
BTHOOM-	Beats the *heck* out of me
BTN-	Better than nothing
BTOIYA-	Be there or it's your *butt*
BTSOOM-	Beats the *crap* out of me
BTTT-	Back to the top / bump to the top
BTW-	By the way
BTWBO-	Be there with bells on
BTWITIAILWU-	By the way I think I am in love with you
BUBU-	Slang for the most beautiful of women
BUH-	Bye-bye
BW-	Best wishes
BWDIK-	But what do I know
BWL-	Bursting with laughter
BWO-	Black, White or Other
BWTM-	But wait, there's more
BYKT-	But you knew that
BYOA-	Bring your own Advil
BYOB-	Bring your own bottle / bring your own beer
BYOBB-	Bring your own brown bag
BYOC-	Bring your own computer
BYOP-	Bring your own paint (paintball)
BYOW-	Build Your Own Website Bring Your Own Wine
BYTM-	Better you than me
BZ-	Busy

C-	See
C YA-	See ya
C&G-	Chuckle and grin
C-P-	Sleepy
C-T-	City
C/P-	Cross Post
C/S-	Change of subject
C4N-	Ciao for now
CAAC-	Cool as a cucumber
CAD-	Control/Alt/Delete
CAD-	Short for Canada/Canadian
CAS-	Crack a smile
CB-	Chat brat/coffee break/call back/crazy*biscuit*
CBARAAHP-	Caught between a rock and a hard place
CBB-	Can't be bothered
CBF-	Can't be *freaked*
CBJ-	Covered blow job
CBL-	Check back later
CBT-	Computer based training/ check back tomorrow
CBWM-	Check back with me
CD9-	Code 9 - it means parents are around
CEO-	Chief Executive Officer
CF-	Coffee *freak*
CFO-	Chief financial officer
CFS-	Care for secret
CFV-	Call for vote
CFY-	Calling for you
CHA-	Click here a-hole
CI-	Check in/ confidential informant

CIAO-	Goodbye (in Italian)
CICO-	Coffee in, coffee out
CICYHW-	Can I copy your homework?
CID-	Consider it done / crying in disgrace
CIL-	Check in later
CLAB-	Crying like a baby
CLM-	Career limiting move
CM-	Call Me
CMAP-	Cover my *butt* partner
CMF-	Count my fingers
CMIIW-	Correct me if I'm wrong
CMON-	Come on
CMU-	Crack me up
CNP-	Continued in next post
COB-	Close of Business
COD-	Change of dressing/ cash on delivery
COF$-	Church of Scientology
COFS-	Church of Scientology
COH-	City of heroes
COS-	Change of subject
CP-	Chat post
CR8-	Create
CRAFT-	Can't remember a *freaking* thing
CRAP-	Cheap redundant assorted products
CRAT-	Can't remember a thing
CRAWS-	Can't remember anything worth a *crap*
CRB-	Come right back
CRBT-	Crying real big tears
CRD-	Caucasian rhythm disorder -or- deficiency
CRDTCHCK-	Credit check
CREAM-	Cash rules everything around me
CRIT-	Critical hit (online gaming)

CRS-	Can't remember *dodo* (stuff)
CRTLA-	Can't remember the three-letter acronym
CS-	Career suicide
CSA-	Cool sweet awesome
CSL-	Can't stop laughing
CSN-	Chuckle, snicker, grin
CSS-	Counter-strike source (online gaming)
CT-	Can't talk
CTA-	Call to action
CTC-	Care to chat /Contact - Choking the chicken
CRHU-	Cracking the *heck* up
CTMQ-	Chuckle to myself quietly
CTO-	Check this out
CU-	See you / cracking up
CU2-	See you too
CUA-	See you around
CUATU-	See you around the universe
CUL-	See you later
CUL8R-	See you later
CULA-	See you later alligator
CUIMD-	See you in my dreams
CUNS-	See you in school
CUOL-	See you online
CURLO-	See you 'round like a donut
CUWTA-	Catch up with the acronyms
CUZ-	Because
CWOT-	Complete waste of time
CWOT&M-	Complete waste of time and money
CWYL-	Chat with you later
CX-	Cancelled
CY-	Calm yourself
CYA-	Cover your *butt* / See ya
CYAL8R-	See you later

CYE-	Check your email
CYEP-	Close your eyes partner (online gaming)
CYL-	See you later
CYM-	Check your mail
CYO-	See you online
CYT-	See you tomorrow

D2-	Dedos/fingers (Spanish sms)
D46?-	Down for sex?
D&M-	Deep & meaningful
D/C-	Disconnected
D00D-	Dude, also seen as dood
DA-	The
DAoC-	Dark Age of Camelot (online gaming)
DAMHIKT-	Don't ask me how I know that
DARFC-	Ducking and running for cover
DBA-	Doing business as
DBAU-	Doing business as usual
DBABAI-	Don't be a *biscuit* about it
DBD-	Don't be dumb
DBEYR-	Don't believe everything you read
DBF-	Divorced black female
DBM-	Divorced black male
DC-	Disconnect/ don't care
DD-	Due diligence/darling daughter/ dear daughter
DDSOS-	Different day, same old *dodo*
DEF-	Definitely
DEGT-	Don't even go there
DEM-	Them
DESE-	These
DETI-	Don't even think it
DEWD-	Dude
DEY-	They
DF-	Dear friend
DFGT-	Don't *freaking* go there

DFL-	Dead *freaking* last
DFLA-	Disenchanted 4-Letter Acronym (that is, a TLA)
DGA-	Don't go anywhere
DGAF-	Don't give a freak
DGT-	Don't go there
DGTG-	Don't go there girlfriend
DGYF-	Damn girl you're fine
DH-	Dear husband
DHC-	Don't hate, congratulate
DHU-	Dinosaur hugs
DHYB-	Don't hold your breath
DIAF-	Die in a fire
DIC-	Drunk in charge
DIIK-	*Darned* if I know
DIKU-	Do I know you?
DILLIGAD-	Do I look like I give a *darn*?
DILLIGAF-	Do I look like I give a *freak*?
DILLIGAS-	Do I look like I give a *dodo*?
DINK-	Double incomes, no kids
DIRFT-	Do it right the first time
DIS-	Did I say/
DISTO-	Did I say that out loud?
DITR-	Dancing in the rain
DITTO-	Same here
DITY-	Did I tell you?
DITYID-	Did I tell you I'm distressed?
DIY-	Do it yourself
DK-	Don't know
DKDC-	Don't know don't care
DKP-	Dragon kill points (online gaming)
DL-	Down low / download / dead link
DLAADS-	Day late and a dollar short

DLTBBB-	Don't let the bed bugs bite
DLTM-	Don't lie to me
DM-	Don't /doesn't matter/direct message/doing me
DMI-	Don't mention it
DN-	Down
DNBL8-	Do not be late
DNC-	Does Not Compute
DND-	Do not disturb
DNR-	Do not repeat/ dinner/ do not reply
DNT-	Don't
DOC-	Drug of choice
DOE-	Depends on experience/ daughter of Eve
DOEI-	Goodbye (in Dutch)
DORD-	Department of Redundancy Department
DP-	Domestic partner/display picture
DPS-	Damage per second
DPYP-	Don't poop your pants
DQMOT-	Don't quote me on this
DQYDJ-	Don't quit your day job
DRB-	Dirty rat bastard
DRIB-	Don't read if busy
DSTR8-	Damn straight
DTC-	Deep throaty chuckle
DTRT-	Do the right thing
DUI-	Driving under the influence
DUM-	Do you masturbate?
DUNA-	Don't use no acronyms
DUNNO-	I don't know
DURS-	*Darn* you are sexy
DUSL-	Do you scream loud?
DUST-	Did you see that?
DW-	Dear/darling wife

DWB-	Don't write back
DWBH-	Don't worry be happy
DWF-	Divorced white female
DWI-	Driving while intoxicated
DWM-	Divorced white male
DWPKOTL-	Deep wet passionate kiss on the lips
DWS-	Driving while stupid
DWWWI-	Surfing the World Wide Web while intoxicated
DWYM-	Do what you mean
DXNRY-	Dictionary
DYFI-	Did you find it?
DYFM-	Dude you fascinate me
DYHAB-	Do you have a boyfriend?
DYHAG-	Do you have a girlfriend?
DYJHIW-	Don't you just hate it when...?
DYLI-	Do you love it?
DYNWUTB-	Do you know what you are talking about?
DYOFDW-	Do your own *freaking* dirty work
DYOR-	Do your own research
DYSTSOTT-	Did you see the size of that thing?

-E-

E	Ecstasy/ enemy (online gaming)
E123-	Easy as one, two, three
E2EG-	Ear to ear grin
E2HO-	Each to his/her own
EAK-	Eating at keyboard
EAPFS-	Everything about Pittsburgh *freaking* sucks
EBKAC-	Error between keyboard and chair
EBT-	Electronic benefits transfer
ED-	Erase display/ electronic discharge
EDP-	Emotionally disturbed person
EE-	Electronic emission
EF4T-	Effort
EFFIN-	*Freaking*
EFT-	Electronic funds transfer
EG-	Evil grin
EI-	Eat it
EIP-	Editing in progress
EL-	Evil laugh
EM-	Excuse me
EMA-	E-mail address
EMFBI-	Excuse me for butting in
EMFJI-	Excuse me for jumping in
EMI-	Excuse my ignorance
EML-	Email me later
EMRTW-	Evil monkey's rule the world
EMSG-	E-mail message
ENUF-	Enough
EO-	Equal opportunity
EOD-	End of day / end of discussion

EOE-	End of era/ equal opportunity employer
EOL-	End of life/ end of lecture
EOM-	End of message
EOS-	End of show/ end of shift
EOT-	End of thread (end of discussion)/end of time
EQ-	Ever Quest (online gaming)
ERS2-	Eres tu/ are you (Spanish sms)
ES-	Erase screen
ESAD-	Eat dodo and die
ESADYFA-	Eat dodo and die you freaking butthole
ESEMED-	Every second every minute every day
ESH-	Experience, strength, and hope
ESMF-	Eat dodo mother *fouler*
ESO-	Equipment smarter than operator
ETA-	Estimated time of arrival -/ edited to add
ETLA-	Extended three-letter acronym (that is, an FLA)
EVA-	Ever
EVERY1-	Everyone
EVRE1-	Everyone
EVO-	Evolution
EWG-	Evil wicked grin (in fun, teasing)
EWI-	E-mailing while intoxicated
EYC-	Excitable, yet calm
EZ-	Easy
EZY-	Easy

F-	Female
F2F-	Face to face
F2P-	Free to play (online gaming)
F8C-	Fake, fraud
FAAK-	Falling asleep at keyboard
FAB-	Features attributes benefits
FAF-	Funny as *freak*
FAH-	*Freaking* a hot
FAP-	*Freaking* a pissed
FAQ-	Frequently asked questions
FAQL-	Frequently asked questions List
FAQOMFT-	Frequently argued waste of my freaking Time
FASB-	Fast *butt* son of *biscuit*
FAWC-	For anyone who cares
FB-	*Freak* buddy
FBI-	*Freaking* brilliant idea / female body inspector
FBI-	Federal Bureau of Investigation
FBF-	Fat boy food (pizza, burgers, fries, etc.)
FBKS-	Failure between keyboard and seat
FBOCD-	Facebook Obsessive Compulsive Disorder
FBOW-	For better or worse
FC-	Fingers crossed/full card (online gaming)
FCFS-	First come, first served
FC'INGOL-	For crying out loud
FCOL-	For crying out loud
FDGB-	Fall down go boom
FE-	Fatal error
FEITCTAJ-	*Freak* 'em if they can't take a joke

FF-	Friends forever
FFA-	Free for all (online gaming)
FF&PN-	Fresh fields and pastures new
FFOD-	Fist full of dollars
FFS-	For *freak* sake
FGDAI-	Fuhgedaboudit / Forget about it
FICCL-	Frankly, I could care less
FIDGAD-	Frankly, I don't give a darn
FIF-	*Freak*, I'm funny
FIFO-	First in, first out
FIGS-	French, Italian, German, Spanish
FIIK-	*Freak*, if I know
FIIOOH-	Forget it, I'm out of here
FIL-	Father-in-law
FILF-	Father I'd like to *freak*
FILTH-	Failed in London, try Hong Kong
FIMH-	Forever in my heart
FINE-	*Freaked* up, Insecure, Neurotic, Emotional
FISH-	First in, still here
FITB-	Fill in the blanks
FLA-	Four Letter Acronym
FLUID-	*Freaking* look it up, I did
FMLTWIA-	*Freak* me like the whore I am
FMTYEWTK-	Far more than you ever wanted to know
FNG-	*Freaking* new guy
FO-	*Freak* off/fell off/ fall out
FOAD-	*Freak* off and die
FOAF-	Friend of a friend
FOAG-	*Freak* off and Google
FOC-	Free of charge
FOFL-	Falling on floor laughing
FOGC-	Fear of getting caught
FOL-	Fond of leather

FOMC-	Fell off my chair
FOMCL-	Falling off my chair laughing
FONE-	Phony
FORD-	Found on road dead /fix or repair daily
FOS-	Full of *dodo*
FRED-	*Freaking* ridiculous electronic device
FRT-	For real, though
FS-	For sale
FSBO-	For sale by owner
FSR-	For some reason
FSU-	*Freak* *crap* up
FT-	Full time/ full term
FTASB-	Faster than a speeding bullet
FTBOMH-	From the bottom of my heart
FTE-	Full time employee
FTF-	*Freak* that's funny / face to face
FTFOI-	For the fun of it / for the freak of it
FTL-	Faster than light
FTLOG-	For the love of God
FTLOI-	For the love of it
FTLOU-	For the love of you
FTN-	*Freak* that noise
FTR-	For the record
FTRF-	*Freak* that's really funny
FTTB-	For the time being
FTW-	For the win / *freak* the world
FU-	*Freak* you
FU2-	*Freak* you too
FUBAR-	*Fouled* up beyond all recognition (or repair)
FUBB-	*Fouled* up beyond belief
FUD-	Fear, uncertainty, & disinformation/face-up deal
FUJIMO-	*Freak* you Jack I'm movin' on

FUM-	*Fouled* up mess
FURTB-	Filled up and ready to burst
FW-	Forward
FWB-	Friends with benefits
FWD-	Forward
FWIW-	For what it's worth
FWM-	Fine with me
FWOT-	*Freaking* waste of time
FYA-	For your amusement
FYD-	Follow your dreams
FYE-	For your edification
FYEO-	For your eyes only
FYF-	From your friend
FYH-	Follow your heart
FYI-	For your information
FYIFV-	*Freak* you I'm fully vested
FYLTGE-	From your lips to God's ears
FYM-	For your misinformation
FYSBIGTBABN-	Fasten your seat belts it's going to be a bumpy night

- G -

G-	Guess / grin / giggle
G1-	Good one
G2CU-	Good to see you
G2G-	Got to go/ good to go
G2GCUL8R-	Got to go see you later
G2GICYAL8R-	Got to go see ya later
G2GLYS-	Got to go love ya so
G2R-	Got to run
G2GT-	Got to get this
G2HI-	Got to have it
G4C-	Going for coffee
G4I-	Go for it
G4N-	Good for nothing
G9-	Genius
GA-	Go ahead
GAB-	Getting a beer
GAD-	Getting a drink
GAFYK-	Get away from your keyboard
GAGFI-	Gives a gay first impression
GAL-	Get a life
GALGAL-	Give a little, get a little
GALHER-	Get a load of her
GALHIM-	Get a load of him
GANB-	Getting another beer
GAP-	Got a picture? / Gay *butt* people
GAS-	Got a second?
GAWD-	God
GB-	God bless/ Good bridge/ goodbye / God body
GBG-	Great big grin

GBH-	Great big hug
GBK-	Great big kiss
GBTW-	Get back to work
GBU-	God bless you
GBWU-	God be with you
GBY-	God bless you
GC-	Good crib
GDR-	Grinning, ducking, running
GD/R-	Grinning, ducking and running
GD&R-	Grinning, ducking and running
GD&RF-	Grinning, ducking and running fast
GDI-	Gosh *darn* it / gosh *darn* independent
GDW-	Grin, duck and wave
G/F-	Girlfriend
GF-	Girlfriend/ ghetto fabulous
GFF-	Go *freaking* figure
GFI-	Go for it
GFM-	God favored/favors me
GFN-	Gone for now
GFON-	Good for one night
GFR-	Grim *fouling* reaper
GFTD-	Gone for the day
GFY-	Good for you /go freak yourself/go find yourself
GFYMF-	Go *freak* yourself mother *fouler*
GG-	Good game / gotta go / Giggling
GGA-	Good game all (online gaming)
GGE1-	Good game everyone (online gaming)
GGG-	Giving God glory
GGGG-	God, God, God, God
GGN-	Gotta go now
GGOH-	Gotta get out of here
GGP-	Give God praise/Gotta go pee

GH-	Good hand (online gaming)/go (going) home
GHM-	God help me
GI-	Google it
GIAR-	Give it a rest
GIC-	Gift in crib/ God's in charge
GIDK-	Gee I don't know
GIG-	God is good
GIGATTIES-	God is good all the time in every situation
GIGO-	Garbage in, garbage out
GIIC-	God is in control
GILF-	Grandmother I'd like to *freak*
GIM-	God in me
GIRL-	Guy in real life
GIWIST-	Gee, I wish I'd said that
GJ-	Good job
GJP-	Good job partner
GL-	Good luck / get lost
GL2U-	Good luck to you
GLA-	Good luck all
GLB-	Good looking boy
GLBT-	Gay, Lesbian, Bisexual, Transgender
GLG-	Good looking girl
GLGH-	Good luck and good hunting
GL/HF-	Good luck, have fun
GLNG-	Good luck, next game (online gaming)
GLYASDI-	God loves you and so do I
GM-	Good morning /good move
GMAB-	Give me a break
GMAFB-	Give me a *freaking* break
GMBA-	Giggling my *butt* off
GMTA-	Great minds think alike
GMTFT-	Great minds think for themselves

GN-	Good night/ go now/got nothing
GNBLFY-	Got nothing but love for you
GNE1-	Good night everyone
GNIGHT-	Good night
GNITE-	Good night
GNOC-	Get naked on cam
GNSD-	Good night sweet dreams
GOI-	Get over it
GOK-	God only knows
GOL-	Giggling out loud
GOOD-	Get out of debt
GOS-	Gay or straight
GOWI-	Get on with it
GOYHH-	Get off your high horse
GP-	General principle/get paid/ getting paid
GR&D-	Grinning, running and ducking
GR2BR-	Good riddance to bad rubbish
GR8-	Great
GRAS-	Generally recognized as safe
GRATZ-	Congratulations
GR&D-	Grinning, running and ducking
GRL-	Girl
GRRLZ-	Girls, also seen as grrl
GRRR-	Growling
GRWG-	Get right with God
GS-	Good shot/good split (online gaming)
GSOAS-	Go sit on a snake
GSOH-	Good sense of humor
GSOAT-	Go sit on a tack
GSYJDWURMNKH-	Good Seeing You, Just Don't Wear Your Monkey Hat
GT-	Good try
GTFO-	Get the *freak* out

GTFOOH-	Get the *freak* out of here
GTG-	Got to go
GTGB-	Got to go, bye
GTGP-	Got to go pee
GTH-	Go to *Hades*
GTK-	Good to know
GTM-	Giggle to myself
GTRM-	Going to read mail
GTSY-	Glad (great or good) to see you
GUD-	Geographically undesirable/ good
GUVMENT-	Government, also seen as guvmint, gumint
GWI-	Get with it
GWS-	Get well soon
GWHTLC-	Glad we had this little chat
GYHOOYA-	Get your head out of your *butt*
GYPO-	Get your pants off

- H -

H-	Hug
H&K-	Hugs and kisses
H/O-	Hold on
H/P-	Hold please
H2CUS-	Hope to see you soon
H4U-	Hot for you
H4XX0R-	Hacker /to be hacked
H8-	Hate
H8TTU-	Hate to be you
H9-	Husband in room
HADVD-	Have Advised
HAG1-	Have a good one
HAGD-	Have a great (good) day
HAGN-	Have a good night
HAGO-	Have a good one
HAK-	Hugs and kisses
HAM-	He's a menace/crazy
HAND-	Have a nice day
HAR-	Hit and run
HAWTLW-	Hello and welcome to last week
HB-	Hurry back/hug back
HBASTD-	Hitting bottom and starting to dig
HBB-	Hip beyond belief
HBIB-	Hot but inappropriate boy
HBIC-	Head biddy in charge
HBU-	How 'bout you?
HCC-	Holy computer crap
HD-	Hold/ help desk

HF-	Hello friend/have fun/have faith/Heavenly Father
HFAC-	Holy flipping animal crackers
HFIG-	Have faith in God
H-FDAY-	Happy Fathers Day
HG-	Holy Ghost
HHIS-	Hanging head in shame
HHO1/2K-	Ha-ha, only half kidding
HHOJ-	Ha-ha, only joking
HHOK-	Ha-ha, only kidding
HHOS-	Ha-ha, only serious
HHTYAY-	Happy Holidays to you and yours
HI 5-	High five
HIG-	How's it going?
HIH-	Hope it helps
HIOOC-	Help, I'm out of coffee
HITAKS-	Hang in there and keep smiling
HL-	Half life (online gaming)
HLA-	Hola/ hello (Spanish sms)
H-MDAY-	Happy Mother's day
HMFIC-	Head *MOFO* in charge
HNL-	(w) hole 'nother level
HNTI-	How nice that/this is
HNTW-	How nice that was
HNY-	Happy New Year
HO-	Hang on / hold on
HOAS-	Hold on a second
HOHA-	Hollywood hacker
HOIC-	Hold on, I'm coming
HOTH-	High on the hog
HOYEW-	Hanging on your every word
HP-	Higher power/hit points/health points (gaming)

HPPO-	Highest paid person in office
HRU-	How are you?
HSIK-	How should I know?
HS-	Holy Spirit
HT-	Hi there
HTB-	Hang the bastards
HTH-	Hope this (or that) helps
HTNOTH-	Hit the nail on the head
HU-	Hook up
HUA-	Heads up ace / head up *butt*
HUB-	Head up *butt*
HUD-	How you doing?
HUGZ-	Hugs
HUH-	What
HUYA-	Head up your *butt*
HV-	Have
HVH-	Heroic Violet hold (online gaming)
HW-	Homework
HWGA-	Here we go again
Hx-	History

⊡Ⅰ⊡

I2-	I too (me too)
I1-D-R-	I wonder
I <3 U-	I love you
I H8 IT-	I hate it
I&I-	Intercourse & inebriation
I-D-L-	Ideal
IA8-	I already ate
IAAA-	I am an accountant
IAAD-	I am a doctor
IAAL-	I am a lawyer
IAC-	In any case / I am confused /if anyone cares
IAE-	In any event
IAITS-	It's all in the subject
IANAC-	I am not a crook
IANADBIPOOTV-	I am not a doctor but I play one on TV
IANAE-	I am not an expert
IANAL-	I am not a lawyer
IANNNGC-	I am not nurturing the next generation of casualties
IAO-	I am out (of here)
IASAP4U-	I always say a prayer for you
IAT-	I am tired
IAW-	I agree with / in accordance with
IAYM-	I am your master
IB-	I'm back
IBGYBG-	I'll be gone, you'll be gone
IBIWISI-	I'll believe it when I see it
IBK-	Idiot behind keyboard
IBRB-	I'll be right back

IBT-	In between technology
IBTC-	Itty bitty titty committee
IBTD-	I beg to differ
IBTL-	In before the lock
IC-	Independent contractor / in character / I See
ICBW-	I could be wrong/ it could be worse
ICBWICBM-	It could be worse, it could be me
ICEDI-	I can't even discuss it
ICFILWU-	I could fall in love with you
ICW-	I can't wait
ICYC-	In case you're curious / in case you care
ID10T-	Idiot
IDC-	I don't care
IDGAD-	I don't give a *darn*
IDGAF-	I don't give a *freak*
IDGARA-	I don't give a rats *butt*
IDGI-	I don't get it /I don't get involved
IDK-	I don't know
IDK, my BFF -	I don't know, my best friend forever
IDKY-	I don't know you
IDM-	It does not matter
IDRK-	I don't really know
IDST-	I didn't say that
IDTA-	I did that already
IDTS-	I don't think so
IDUNNO-	I don't know
IEF-	It's Esther's fault
IF/IB-	In the front / in the back
IFAB-	I found a bug
IFU-	I *fouled* up
IFYP-	I feel your pain
IG2R-	I got to run

IGG-	I gotta go
IGGP-	I gotta go pee
IGGUS-	I'm gonna get you sucker
IGHT-	I got high tonight
IGN-	I (I've) got nothing
IGP-	I got to (go) pee
IGTP-	I get the point
IGTV-	I got the victory
IGWS-	It goes without saying
IGWST-	It goes without saying that
IGWT-	In God we trust
IGYHTBT-	I guess you had to be there
IHA-	I hate acronyms
IHAIM-	I have another instant message
IHNI-	I have no idea
IHNO-	I have no opinion
IHTFP-	I have truly found paradise / I hate this freaking place
IHU-	I hear you
IIABDFI-	If it ain't broke, don't fix it
IIIO-	Intel inside, idiot outside
IIMAD-	If it makes an(y) difference
IINM-	If I'm not mistaken
IIR-	If I remember /If I recall
IIRC-	If I remember correctly / If I recall correctly
IIT-	Is it tight?
IITLYTO-	If it's too loud you're too old
IITYWIMWYBMAD-	If I tell you what it means will you buy me a drink
IITYWYBMAD-	If I tell you will you buy me a drink?
IIWM-	If it were me
IJPMP-	I just pissed my pants

IJWTK-	I just want to know
IJWTS-	I just want to say
IK-	I know
IKALOPLT-	I know a lot of people like that
IKR-	I know, right?
IKWYM-	I know what you mean
IKYABWAI-	I know you are but what am I?
ILA-	I love acronyms
ILBL8-	I'll be late
ILF/MD-	I love female/male dominance
ILI-	I'm loving it
ILICISCOMK-	I laughed, I cried, I spat/spilt coffee/crumbs/coke on my keyboard
ILMJ-	I love my job
ILU-	I love you
ILUAAF-	I love you as a friend
ILUM-	I love you man (much/more)
ILY-	I love you
IM-	Instant messaging /immediate message
IM2BZ2P-	I am too busy to (even) pee
IMA-	I might add
IMAO-	In my arrogant opinion
IMCO-	In my considered opinion
IME-	In my experience
IMEZRU-	I am easy, are you?
IMHEIUO-	In my high exalted informed unassailable opinion
IMHO-	In my humble opinion
ImL-	I love you (using American sign language)
IMNERHO-	In my never even remotely humble opinion
IMNSHO-	In my not so humble opinion
IMO-	In my opinion

IMOO-	In my own opinion
IMPOV-	In my point of view
IMRU-	I am, are you?
IMS-	I am sorry
IMSB-	I am so bored
IMTM-	I am the man
IMTW-	I am the woman
INAL-	I'm not a lawyer
INBD-	It's no big deal
INC-	Incoming (online gaming)
INMP-	It's not my problem
INNW-	If not now, when
INPO-	In no particular order
INUCOSM-	It's no use crying over spilt milk
IOH-	I'm outta here
IOMH-	In over my head
ION-	Index of names
IONO-	I don't know
IOU-	I owe you
IOUD-	Inside, outside, upside down
IOW-	In other words
IP4U-	I'll pray for you
IPN-	I'm posting naked
IRL-	In real life
IRMC-	I rest my case
ISAGN-	I see a great need
ISH-	Insert sarcasm here
ISLY-	I still love you
ISO-	In search of
ISS-	I said so / I'm so sure
ISSYGTI-	I'm so sure you get the idea
ISTM-	It seems to me

ISTR-	I seem to remember
ISWC-	If stupid was a crime
ISWYM-	I see what you mean
ISYALS-	I'll send you a letter soon
ITA-	I totally agree
ITAM-	It's the Accounting man (financial blogs)
ITFA-	In the final analysis
ITIGBS-	I think I'm going to be sick
ITM-	In the money
ITMA-	It's that man again
ITS-	Intense text sex
ITSFWI-	If the shoe fits wear it
ITYK-	I thought you knew
IUM-	If you must
IUSS-	If you say so
IWALU-	I will always love you
IWAWO-	I want a way out
IWBNI-	It would be nice if
IWBTL-	I will bless the Lord
IWBTLAAT-	I will bless the Lord at all times
IWFU-	I wanna *freak* you
IWIAM-	Idiot wrapped in a moron
IWIWU-	I wish I was you
IWSN-	I want sex now
IYAOYAS-	If you ain't ordinary you ain't *crap*
IYD-	In your dreams
IYDMMA-	If you don't mind my asking
IYFEG-	Insert your favorite ethnic group
IYKWIM-	If you know what I mean
IYKWIMAITYD-	If you know what I mean and I think you do
IYO-	In your opinion
IYQ-	I like you

IYSS- If you say so
IYSWIM- If you see what I mean

-J-

J/C-	Just checking
J/J-	Just joking
J/K-	Just kidding
J/O-	Jerking off/ jerk off
J/P-	Just playing
J/W-	Just wondering
J00-	You
J00R-	Your
J2LYK-	Just to let you know
J4F-	Just for fun
J4G-	Just for grins
J4T /JFT-	Just for today
J5M-	Just five minutes
JAC-	Just a sec
JAD-	Just another day
JAFO-	Just another *freaking* onlooker
JAFS-	Just a *freaking* salesman
JAM-	Just a minute
JAS-	Just a second
JC-	Just curious / just chilling / Jesus Christ
JDI-	Just do it
JDMJ-	Just doing my job
JEOMK-	Just ejaculated on my keyboard
JFF-	Just for fun
JFGI-	Just *freaking* Google it
JFH-	Just *freak* her/ just for her
JFI-	Just for information
JHO-	Just helping out
JHOM-	Just helping out my (mafia, mob, neighbors, etc.)

JHOMF-	Just helping out my friend(s)
JIC-	Just in case
JJA-	Just joking around
JK-	Just kidding
JLMK-	Just let me know
JM2C-	Just my 2 cents
JMO-	Just my opinion
JOOTT-	Just one of those things
JP-	Just playing/ jackpot (online gaming)
JSU-	Just shut up
JSYK-	Just so you know
JT-	Just teasing
JTLYK-	Just to let you know
JTOL-	Just thinking out loud
JTOU-	Just thinking of you
JUADLAM-	Jumping up and down like a monkey
JW-	Just wondering

K-	Okay/ ok
KK-	Kiss, kiss
KK-	Knock, knock/ okay, okay
K8T-	Katie
KB-	Kick butt
KBD-	Keyboard
KDFU-	Cracked the *freak* up
KEWL-	Cool
KEYA-	Key you later
KEYME-	Key me when you get in
KFY /K4Y-	Kiss for you
KHYF-	Know how you feel
KIA-	Killed in action/ know it all
KIBO-	Knowledge in, *bull-crap* out
KIR-	Keep it real
KISS-	Keep it simple stupid
KIT-	Keep in touch
KITTY-	Code word for vagina
KMA-	Kiss my *butt*
KMBA-	Kiss my black *butt*
KMFHA-	Kiss my fat hairy *butt*
KMP-	Keep me posted
KMRIA-	Kiss my royal Irish *butt*
KMSLA-	Kiss my shiny little *butt*
KMUF-	Kiss me you fool
KMWA-	Kiss my white *butt*
KO-	Knock out
KOK-	Knock

KOL-	Kiss on lips
KOTC-	Kiss on the cheek
KOTL-	Kiss on the lips
KPC-	Keeping parents clueless
KR-	Kick rocks
KS-	Kill stealer/ kill then steal (online gaming)
KT-	Katie
KUTGW-	Keep up the good work
KWIM-	Know what I mean?
KWSTA-	Kiss with serious tongue action
KYFC-	Keep your fingers crossed
KYPO-	Keep your pants on

L-	Laugh
L2G-	Like to go / Love to go
L2K-	Like to come
L33T-	Leet, meaning elite
L8R-	Later
L?^-	Let's hook up
LABATYD-	Life's a *biscuit* and then you die
LAIC-	Large and in charge
LAQ-	Lame butt quote
LASJC-	Lord and Savior Jesus Christ
LATWTTB-	Laughing all the way to the bank
LB?W/C-	Like bondage? Whips or chains
LBIG-	Laughing because I'm gay
LBR /LGR-	Little boy's room / little girl's room
LBUG-	Laughing because you're gay
LD-	Long distance / later dude
LDIMEDILLIGAF-	Look deeply into my eyes, does it look like I give a *freak*?
LDR-	Long distance relationship
LDTTWA-	Let's do the time warp again
LEMENO-	Let me know
LEMOI-	Loving every minute of it
LERK-	Leaving easy reach of keyboard
LF-	Let's *freak*
LFG-	Looking for group/guard (online gaming)
LFM-	Looking for more (online gaming)
LFTI-	Looking forward to it
LG-	Life's good/ let God

LGLG-	Let go let God
LGMAS-	Lord, give me a sign
LHM-	Lord, have mercy
LHO-	Laughing head off
LHOS-	Let's have online sex
LHSO-	Let's have sex online
LHU-	Let's hook up
LIC-	Like I care
LIK-	Liquor
LIFO-	Last in, first out
LIMT-	Laughing in my tummy
LIS-	Laughing in silence
LJBF-	Let's just be friends
LKITR-	Little kid in the room
LL-	Living large/loving life
LLGB-	Love, later, God bless
LLOM-	Like Leno on meth
LLTA-	Lots and lots of thunderous applause
LMAO-	Laughing my *butt* off
LMBO-	Laughing my butt off
LMFAO-	Laughing my *freaking* *butt* off
LMHO-	Laughing my head off
LMIRL-	Let's meet in real life
LMK-	Let me know
LMNK-	Leave my name out
LMNO-	Leave my name out
LMSO-	Laughing my socks off
LMTC-	Left a message to contact
LMTCB-	Left message to call back
LNT-	Lost in translation
LOA-	List of acronyms
LOL-	Laughing (laugh) out loud / lots of love

LOLA-	Laugh out loud again
LOL☺-	Laughing out loud grinning
LOLWTF-	Laughing out loud, what the *freak*?
LOLZ-	Lots of laughs
LOMBARD-	Lots of money but a right *ding-a-ling*
LOML-	Love of my life
LONH-	Lights on, nobody home
LOOL-	Laughing outrageously out loud
LOP-	Living on purpose
LOPSOD-	Long on promises, short on delivery
LORE-	Learn once, repeat everywhere
LOTI-	Laughing on the inside
LOTOTW-	Live on top of the world
LOTR-	Lord of the rings (online gaming)
LOU-	Laughing over you
LPOS-	Lazy piece of *crap*
LQTM-	Laughing quietly to myself
LRF-	Little rubber feet
LSHITIPAL-	Laughing so hard I think I peed a little
LSHMBH-	Laughing so hard my belly hurts
LSTTB-	Laughing straight to the bank
LSV-	Language, sex, violence
LYBL-	Living the blessed life
LTD-	Living the dream
LTHTT-	Laughing too hard to type
LTIC-	Laughing till I cry
LTIO-	Laughing till I orgasm
LTLWDLS-	Let's twist like we did last summer
LTM-	Laughing to myself
LTNS-	Long time no see
LTNT-	Long time, no type
LTOD-	Laptop of death

LTR-	Long term relationship
LTS-	Laughing to self
LTTIC-	Look the teacher is coming
LULT-	Love you long time
LULU-	Locally undesirable land use
LULZ-	Slang for LOL
LUMTP-	Love you more than pie
LUSER-	Loser
LUSM-	Love you so much
LWR-	Launch when ready
LY-	Love you/ love ya
LY4E-	Love you forever
LYA-	Love you all
LYB-	Love you babe
LYLC-	Love you like crazy
LYCYLBB-	Love you, see you later, bye-bye
LYKYAMY-	Love you, kiss you, already miss you
LYL-	Love you lots
LYLAB-	Love you like a brother
LYLAS-	Love you like a sister
LYLB-	Love you, later, bye
LYMI-	Love you, mean it
LYSM-	Love you so much
LYWAMH-	Love you with all my heart

M2NY-	Me too, not yet
M4C-	Meet for coffee
M4W-	Men for women
M8 / M8S-	Mate / mates
MA-	Mature audience/ make available
MAYA-	Most Advanced Yet Accessible
MB-	Message board/mama's boy
MBN-	Must be nice
MBRFN-	Must be real *freaking* nice
MD-	Medical doctor /managing director/make direct
MEGO-	My eyes glaze over
MEH-	Meaning so-so/ just ok/who cares, whatever
MEHH-	Meaning sigh or sighing
MEZ-	Mesmerize
MF-	My Friend
MFD-	Multi-Function Device
MFG-	Mit freundlichen Gruessen (German) meaning- With friendly greetings or yours sincerely
MFI-	Mad for it/ made for it
MFIC-	Mother *fouler* in charge
MFWIC-	Mo *fouler* who's in charge
MGB-	May God bless
MGBAKY-	May God bless and keep you
MGBY-	May God bless you
MGBYRG-	May God bless you real good
MGBWU-	May God be with you
MGBWYA-	May God be with you always
MHBFY-	My heart bleeds for you
MHHM-	Uh huh / yeah

MHOTY-	My hat's off to you
MIA-	Missing in action
MIHAP-	May I have your attention please
MIL-	Mother-In-Law
MILF-	Mother I'd like to *freak*
MIRL-	Meet in real life
MITIN-	More info than I needed
MKOP-	My kind of place
MLA-	Multiple letter acronyms
MLAS-	My lips are sealed
MLM-	Giving the digital middle finger
MM-	Market maker/money maker/sister -Mandarin
MMC-	Made me cry
MMD-	Make (made) my day
MMDAR-	Make my dreams a reality
MMHA2U-	My most humble apologies to you
MMK-	Mmm ok
MKAY-	Meaning Mmm, okay
MML-	Made me laugh
MMM-	Made me mad
MMMU-	My mind's made up
MMYT-	Mail me your thoughts
MNC-	Mother Nature calls
MNSG-	Mensaje (message in Spanish)
MO-	Move on/ mode of operation/ modus operandi
MOF-	Matter of fact
MOFO-	Mother *fouler*
MOM-	Mind over matter
MOMBOY-	Mama's boy
MOMPL-	One moment please
MOO-	Mud, object-oriented / matter of opinion
MOOS-	Member of the opposite sex
MOP-	Moment please

M/F-	Male or female
MorF-	Male or female
MOS-	Mom (mother) over shoulder
MOSS-	Member(s) of the same sex
MOTAS-	Member of the appropriate sex
MOTD-	Message of the day
MOTOS-	Member(s) of the opposite sex
MOTSS-	Member(s) of the same sex
MP-	Military police/ mana points (online gaming)
MPFB-	My personal *freak* buddy
MRA-	Moving right along
MRPH-	Mail the right place for help
MSG-	Message
MSMD-	Monkey see monkey do
MSNUW-	Mini-skirt no under-wear
MSTM-	Makes sense to me
MTBF-	Mean time before failure
MTF-	More to follow
MTFBWU-	May the force be with you
MTFBWY-	May the force be with you
MTLA-	My true love always
MTSBWY-	May the Schwartz be with you
MUAH-	Multiple unsuccessful attempts
MUAH -	The sound of a kiss
MWAH-	The sound of a kiss
MUBAR-	Messed up beyond all recognition
MUSL-	Missing you *crap* loads
MUSM-	Miss you so much
MVA-	Motor vehicle accident
MVA no PI-	Motor vehicle accident with no personal injury
MVA w/PI-	Motor vehicle accident with personal injury
MWBRL-	More will be revealed later
MYB-	Mind your business

MYL-	Mind your language
MYM-	Mind your manners
MYO-	Mind your own
MYOB-	Mind your own business

NA-	Not applicable
N-	No
N-A-Y-L-	In a while
N/A-	Not applicable /not affiliated
N/M-	Nothing much
N/T-	No text
N00B-	Newbie
N1-	Nice one/ no one
N2M	Not to mention/not too much/nothing too much
N2MJCHBU-	Not too much just chillin', how 'bout you?
NAB-	Not a blonde
NADT-	Not a *darn* thing
NAGB-	Nearly almost a good bridge
NAK-	Nursing at keyboard
NALOPKT-	Not a lot of people know that
NANA-	Not now, no need
NASCAR-	Non-athletic sport centered around rednecks
NATCH-	Naturally
NATO-	No action, talk only
NAVY-	Never again volunteer yourself
NAZ-	Name, Address, and Zip (also means Nasdaq)
NB-	Never been, Nota Bene- meaning take notice of this very carefully- Latin
NB4T-	Not before time
NBD-	No big deal
NBFAB-	Not bad for a beginner
NBFABS-	Not bad for a bot stopper
NBG-	No bloody good
NBIF-	No basis in fact

NBLFY-	Nothing but love for you
NBS-	No bull *crap*
NC-	Nice crib
NCG-	New college graduate
NCNS-	No call no show/no complications/ no sequel
ND-	No date/ no deal/no double (online gaming)
NDN-	Indian
NE-	Any
NE-WAYZ-	Anyways
NE1-	Anyone
NE14KFC-	Anyone for KFC?
NE1ER-	Anyone here?
NE2H-	Need To Have
NEET-	Not currently engaged in employment, education, or training
NESEC-	Any second
NEV-	Neighborhood electric vehicle
NEWS-	North, East, West, South
NFBSK-	Not for British school kids
NFC-	Not favorably considered/No *freaking* chance
NFF-	No *freaking* fair
NFG-	Not *freaking* good
NFI-	No *freaking* Idea
NFM-	Not for me
NFS-	Need for sex / network files system/ need for speed/ not for sale
NFW-	No *freaking*way/No feasible way/not for work
NFWS-	Not for work safe
NG-	New game
NGB-	Nearly good bridge
NH-	Nice hand
NHOH-	Never heard of him/her

NI4NI-	An eye for any eye
NICE-	Nonsense in crappy existence
NIFOC-	Nude (naked) in front of the computer
NIGI-	Now I get it
NIGYYSOB-	Now I've got you, you son of a *biscuit*
NIH-	Not invented here
NIM-	No internal message
NIMBY-	Not in my back yard
NIMJD-	Not in my job description
NIMQ-	Not in my queue
NIMY-	Never in a million years
NINO-	Nothing in, nothing out / no input, no output
NISM-	Need I say more
NITL-	Not in this lifetime
NIYWFD-	Not in your wildest *freaking* dreams
NLL-	Nice little lady
NM-	Never mind /nothing much / nice move
NMH-	Not much here
NMU-	Not much, you?
NME-	Enemy
NMH-	Not much here
NMHJC-	Not much here, just chilling
NMP-	Not my problem
NMTE-	Now more than ever
NMU-	Not much, you?
NN-	Not now /no need
NNCIMINTFZ-	Not now chief, I'm in the *freaking* zone
NNDMN-	Not now doesn't mean never
NNR-	Need not respond
NNWW-	Nudge, nudge, wink, wink
NO-	Not online/ no one
NO PRAW-	No problem

NOA-	Not online anymore
NOFI-	No offence intended
NOOB-	Someone who is bad at online games
NOS-	New old stock
NOY-	Not online yet
NOYB-	None of your business
NP-	No problem / nosy parents
NPC-	Non-playing character (online gaming)
NQA-	No questions asked
NQT-	Newly qualified teacher
NQOCD-	Not quite our class dear
NR-	Nice roll/ no reason/ not really
NRG-	Energy
NRN-	No reply necessary
NS-	Nice set/nice score/ nice split (online gaming)
NSA-	No strings attached
NSFW-	Not safe for work
NSISR-	Not sure if spelled right
NSS-	No *crap* Sherlock
NSTLC-	Need some tender loving care
NT-	Nice try/ not there/next time
NTA-	Not this again
NTH-	Nothing
NTHING-	Nothing
NTIM-	Not that it matters
NTIMM-	Not that it matters much
NTK-	Nice To Know
NTM-	Not that much
NTMU-	Nice to meet you
NTTAWWT-	Not that there's anything wrong with that
NTW-	Not to worry
NTYMI-	Now that you mention it

NUB-	New person to a site or game
NUFF-	Enough
NUFFS-	Enough said
NVM-	Never mind
NVR-	Never
NVNG-	Nothing ventured, nothing gained
NW-	No way
NWAL-	Nerd without a life
NWO-	No way out
NWOT-	New without tags
NWR-	Not work related
NWT-	New with tags
NYC-	Not your concern/New York City
NYCFS-	New York City finger salute

O4U-	Only for you
O-	Opponent / over/ hugs
OA-	Online auctions
OAO-	Over and out
OATUS-	On a totally unrelated subject
OAUS-	On an unrelated subject
OB-	Oh baby/oh brother/ obligatory
OBE-	Overcome by events
OBO-	Or best offer
OBTW-	Oh by the way
OBX-	Old battle axe
OC-	Original character / own character
OCD-	Obsessive compulsive disorder
ODTAA-	One darn thing after another
OI-	Operator indisposed
OIC-	Oh, I see
OICU812-	Oh I see you ate one, too
OJ-	Only joking/ orange juice
OK-	Okay/all correct
OL-	Old Lady
OLL-	Online love
OLN-	Online netiquette
OLO-	Only laughed once
OM-	Old man/ oh my
OMB-	Oh my Buddha/ oh my brother
OMDB-	Over my dead body
OMFG-	Oh my *freaking* God
OMG-	Oh my God (gosh)

OMGYG2BK-	Oh my God, you got to be kidding
OMIK-	Open mouth, insert keyboard
OML-	Oh my Lord
OMO-	On my own
OMW-	On my way
ONID-	Oh no, I didn't
ONHD-	Oh no, he didn't
ONL-	Online
ONNA-	Oh no, not again
ONSD-	Oh no, she didn't
ONNTA-	Oh no, not this again
ONUD-	Oh no, you didn't
OO-	Over and out
OOAK-	One of a kind
OOB-	Out of box
OOC-	Out of character / out of control
OOF-	Out of facility
OOI-	Out of interest
OOO-	Out of office
OOS-	Out of stock
OOTB-	Out of the box / out of the blue
OOTC-	Obligatory on topic comment
OOTD-	One of those days
OOTO-	Out of the office
OP-	On purpose/on phone
ORLY-	Oh really
OSIF-	Oh *sugar* I forgot
OSINTOT-	Oh *sugar* I never thought of that
OST-	On second thought
OT-	Off topic
OTASOIC-	Owing to a slight oversight in construction
OTB-	Off to bed

OTC-	Over the counter
OTF-	Off the floor / on the phone (fone)
OTH-	Off the hook
OTL-	Out to lunch/crazy
OTOH-	On the other hand
OTOTW-	On top of the world
OTP-	On the phone
OTT-	Over the top
OTTOMH-	Off the top of my head
OTW-	Off the wall/ over the wire/ off to work
OUSU-	Oh, you shut up
OVA-	Over
OWTTE-	Or words to that effect
OYO-	On your own
OZ-	Australia

P-	Partner
P&C-	Private & confidential
P-ZA-	Pizza
P2C2E-	Process too complicated to explain
P2U4URAQTP-	Peace to you for you are a cutie pie
P2P-	Peer to peer/pay to play/parent to parent
P4M-	Pray for me
P911-	Parent alert
PA-	Parent alert
PAL-	Parents are listening
PANS-	Pretty awesome new stuff
PAW-	Parents are watching
PB-	Potty break
PBB-	Parent behind back
PBEM-	Play by email
PBIAB-	Pay back is a *biscuit*
PBJ-	Peanut butter and jelly / pretty boy jock
PBOOK-	Phonebook
PC-	Personal computer / politically correct
PCM-	Please call me
PCMCIA-	People can't memorize computer industry acronyms
PD-	Public domain/personal day
PDA-	Personal digital assistant / Public display of affection
PDOMA-	Pulled directly out of my *butt*
PDH-	Pretty *darn* happy
PDQ-	Pretty *darn* quick

PDS-	Please don't shout/please don't shoot
PEBCAC-	Problem exists between chair and computer
PEBCAK-	Problem exists between chair and keyboard
PEEP-	People Engaged and Empowered for Peace
PEEPS-	People
PFA-	Pulled from *butt* / please find attached
PFC-	Pretty *freaking* cold
PFT-	Pretty *freaking* tight
PH-	Praise him
PHAT-	Pretty hot and tempting
PHB-	Pointy haired boss
PHIA-	Praise him in advance
PHN-	Praise him now
PHS-	Pointy haired stupid-visor
PIAPS-	Pig in a pant suit
PIBKAC-	Problem is between keyboard and chair
PIC-	Picture
PICNIC-	Problem in chair, not in computer
PIF-	Paid in full
PIMP-	Peeing in my pants
PIMPL-	Peeing in my pants laughing
PIN-	Person in need
PIR-	Parent in room
PITA-	Pain in the *butt*
PITMEMBOAM-	Peace in the Middle East my brother of another mother
PIX-	Pictures / photos
PKMN-	Pokémon (online gaming)
PL8-	Plate
PLD-	Played
PLMK-	Please let me know
PLO-	Peace, love, out

PLOKTA-	Press lots of keys to abort
PLOS-	Parents looking over shoulder
PLS-	Please
PLU-	People like us
PLZ-	Please
PM-	Personal message / private message
PMBI-	Pardon my butting in
PMF-	Pardon my French / pure *freaking* magic
PMFI-	Pardon me for interrupting
PMFJI-	Pardon me for jumping in
PMIGBOM-	Put mind in gear before opening mouth
PMJI-	Pardon my jumping in
PML-	Pissing myself laughing
PMP-	Peeing my pants
PMSL-	Pissed myself laughing
PNATMBC-	Pay no attention to man behind the curtain
PNCAH-	Please, no cursing allowed here
PND-	Possibly not definitely/personal navigation device
PO-	Piss off
POAHF-	Put on a happy face
POAK-	Passed out at keyboard
POI-	Point of interest/place of interest/person of interest
POMS-	Parent over my shoulder
PONA-	Person of no account
PONR-	Point of no return
POP-	Photo on profile /point of purchase / point of presence / post office protocol
POS-	Parent over shoulder / piece of *stinky*
POSC-	Piece of *sugar* computer
POSSLQ-	Persons of the opposite sex sharing living quarters

POTATO-	Person over thirty acting twenty one
POTS-	Plain old telephone system/pat on the shoulder
POTUS-	President of the United States
POV-	Point of view/ privately owned vehicle
PP-	People
PPL-	Pay-per-lead /people
PPU-	Pending pick-up
PROGGY-	Program (programming)
PROLLY-	Probably
PRON-	Porn (pornography)
PRT-	Party
PRW-	Parents are watching/people are watching
PS-	Post script
PSA-	Public service announcement
PSO-	Product superior to operator
PSOS-	Parents standing over shoulder
PSP-	Play station portable
PST-	Please send tell (online gaming)
PTH-	Prime tanning hours
PTL-	Praise the Lord
PTMM-	Please tell me more
PTP-	Pardon the pun
PTPOP-	Pat the pissed off primate
PU-	That stinks
P/U-	Pick up
PUG-	Pick up group (online gaming)
PUKS-	Pick up kids
PUTER-	Computer
PVP-	Player versus player
PW-	Password
PWAS-	Prayer wheels are spinning
PWCB-	Person will call back

PWN-	Own
PWNT-	Owned
PWP-	Plot, what plot?
Px-	Prescriptions
PXT-	Please explain that
PZ-	Peace
PZA-	Pizza

[-]@[-]

Q-	Queue / question
Q2C-	Quick to cum
QC-	Quality control
QFE-	Question for everyone
QFI-	Quoted for idiocy/quoted for irony
QFT-	Quoted for truth / quit *freaking* talking
QIK-	Quick
QL-	Quit laughing
QLS-	Reply
QOTD-	Quote of the day/question of the day
QPQ-	Quid pro quo
QQ-	Quick question / cry more/crying eyes
QS-	Quit scrolling
QSL-	Reply
QSO-	Conversation
QT-	Cutie
QTPI-	Cutie pie
QYB-	Quit your *biscuit*

- R -

R8-	Rate
R-	Are
R U DA?-	Are you there?
R U GOIN-	Are you going?
R U THERE?-	Are you there?
R&D-	Research & development
R&R-	Rest & relaxation
RAEBNC-	Read and enjoyed, but no comment
RAT-	Remotely activated Trojan
RB@YA-	Right back at ya
RBAY-	Right back at you
RBTL-	Read between the lines
RC-	Remote control
RCI-	Rectal cranial inversion
RD-	Riding dirty
RE-	Regards / reply / hello again
REHI-	Hi again
RFD-	Request for discussion
RFR-	Really *freaking* rich
RFS-	Really *freaking* soon
RGR-	Roger
RHIP-	Rank has its privileges
RHK-	Roundhouse kick
RIP-	Rest in peace
RIYL-	Recommended if you like
RKBA-	Right to keep and bear arms
RL-	Real life
RLCO-	Real life conference

RLF-	Real life friend
RM-	Remake
RME-	Rolling my eyes
RMETTH-	Rolling my eyes towards the heavens
RML-	Read my lips
RMLB-	Read my lips baby
RMM-	Read my mind
RMMA-	Reading my mind again
RMMM-	Read my mail man
RN-	Right now
RNN-	Reply not necessary
ROFL-	Rolling on floor laughing
ROFLCOPTER-	Rolling on floor laughing spinning around
ROR-	Raffing out roud (in scooby-doo dialect)
ROT-	Right on time
ROTFL-	Rolling on the floor laughing
ROTFLMAO-	Rolling on the floor laughing my *butt* off
ROTFLMFAO-	Rolling on the floor laughing my *freaking* *butt* off
ROTFLOL-	Rolling on the floor laughing out loud
ROTFLUTS-	Rolling on the floor laughing unable to speak
ROTGL-	Rolling on the ground laughing
ROTGLMAO-	Rolling on the ground laughing my *butt* off
ROTM-	Right on the money
RPG-	Role playing games
RRQ-	Return receipt requested
RRR-	HaR haR haR (instead of LOL)
RS-	Runescape (online gaming)/ running scared
RSN-	Real soon now
RSVP-	Repondez S'il Vous Plait- please reply
RT-	Real time
RTB-	Returning to base (home)

RTBM-	Read the bloody manual
RTBS-	Reason to be single
RTFAQ-	Read the FAQ
RTFF-	Read the *freaking* FAQ
RTFM-	Read the *freaking* manual
RTFQ-	Read the *freaking* question
RTH-	Release the hounds
RTK-	Return to keyboard
RTM -	Read the manual
RTMS-	Read the manual stupid
RTNTN-	Retention email (Government)
RTRCTV-	Retroactive email (Government)
RTRMT-	Retirement email (Government)
RTS-	Read the screen/return to sender
RTSM-	Read the silly/stupid manual
RTSS-	Read the screen stupid
RTTS-	Right thing to say
RTTSD-	Right thing to say dude
RTWG-	Round the way girl
RTWFQ-	Read the whole *freaking* question
RU-	Are you?
RU/18-	Are you over 18?
RUFKM-	Are you *freaking* kidding me?
RUH-	Are you horny?
RUMCYMHMD-	Are you on medication cause you must have missed a dose
RUMOF-	Are you male or female?
RUNTS-	Are you nuts?
RUOK-	Are you ok?
RUS-	Are you serious?
RUSOS-	Are you SOS (in trouble)?
RUT-	Are you there?

RUUP4IT-	Are you up for it?
RX-	Regards/drugs
RYB-	Read your bible
RYFM-	Read your friendly manual
RYO-	Roll your own
RYS-	Read your screen/ are you single

- S -

S-	Smile
S2MG-	Sticking to my guns
S2R-	Send to receive
S2S-	Sorry to say
S2U-	Same to you
S4B-	*Sugar* for brains
S4L-	Spam for life
SADAD-	Suck a *ding a ling* and die
SAHM-	Stay at home mom
SAIA-	Stupid *butts* in action
SAL-	Such a laugh
SALM4U-	Saving all my love for you
SAPFU-	Surpassing all previous foul ups
SAS-	Saved and sanctified
SASFWTHG-	Save and sanctified filled with the Holy Ghost
SB-	Stand by
SBF-	Single black female
SBI-	Sorry 'bout it
SBM-	Single black male
SBT-	Sorry 'bout that
SBTA-	Sorry, being thick again
SBUG-	Small bald un-audacious goal
SC-	Stay cool/ so cool
SCNR-	Sorry, could not resist
SDK-	Scottie doesn't know / software developer's kit
SDMB-	Sweet dreams, my baby
SEC-	Wait a second
SED-	Said enough darling

SEG-	*Sugar* eating grin
SEP-	Somebody else's problem
SETE-	Smiling ear to ear
SEWAG-	Scientifically engineered wild *butt* guess
SF-	Surfer friendly / science fiction/ Spirit filled
SFAIAA-	So, far as I am aware
SFAIK-	So, far as I know
SFETE-	Smiling from ear to ear
SFLA-	Stupid four letter acronym
SFLW-	Stupid four letter word
SFTTM-	Stop *freaking* talking to me
SFX-	Sound effects / stage effects/special effects
SH-	*Poop* happens/ same here
SH^-	Shut up
SHB-	Should have been
SHHH-	Quiet
SHID-	Slap head in disgust
SHMILY-	See how much I love you
SI-	Simply irresistible
SIC-	Spelling is correct
SICL-	Sitting in chair laughing
SICNR-	Sorry I could not resist
SICS-	Sitting in chair snickering
SIG2R -	Sorry, I got to run
SIHTH-	Stupidity is hard to take
SII-	Seriously impaired imagination
SIL-	Sister-in-Law
SIMYC-	Sorry, I missed your call
SIP-	Skiing in powder
SIR-	Strike it rich
SIS-	Snickering in silence
SIT-	Stay in touch

SITCOM-	Single income, two children, oppressive mortgage
SITD-	Still in the dark
SIUP-	Suck it up *kitty*
SIUYA-	Shove it up your *booty*
SK8-	Skate
SK8ER-	Skater
SK8NG-	Skating
SK8R-	Skater
SK8RBOI-	Skater boy
SL-	Second life
SLAP-	Sounds like a plan
SLAW-	Sounds like a winner
SLIRK-	Smart little rich kid
SLM-	See last mail
SLOM-	Sticking leeches on myself
SLT-	Something like that
SM-	Senior moment/smart move
SMAIM-	Send me an instant message
SMB-	Suck my balls
SME-	Subject matter expert
SMEM-	Send me e-mail
SMH-	Shaking my head
SMHID-	Scratching my head in disbelief
SMIM-	Send me an instant message
SMOP-	Small matter of programming
SMT-	Something
SNAFU-	Situation normal, all *fouled* up
SNAG-	Sensitive new age guy
SNERT-	Snotty nosed egotistical rotten teenager
SO-	Significant other
SOB-	Son of a *biscuit*
SOBT-	Stressed out big time

SODDI-	Some other dude did it
SOGOP-	*Poop* or get off the pot
SOH-	Sense of humor
SOHF-	Sense of humor failure
SOI-	Self owning idiot
SOIAR-	Sit on it and rotate
S'OK-	It's ok
SOK-	It's ok
SOL-	*Poop* out of luck/ sooner or later
SOME1-	Someone
SOMY-	Sick of me yet
SOOYA-	Snake out of your *booty*
SOP-	Standard operating procedure/stand on principles
SorG-	Straight or gay
SOS-	Same old *sugar*/ help/ son of Sam
SOT-	Short on time
SOTMG-	Short on time, must go
SOW-	Speaking of which/statement of work
SOWM-	Someone with me
SOZ-	Sorry
SPK-	Speak
SPST-	Same place, same time
SPTO-	Spoke to
SQ-	Square
SRO-	Standing room only/something really outrageous
SRSLY-	Seriously
SRY-	Sorry
SS-	So sorry
SSASF-	Saved, sanctified and Spirit filled
SSC-	Super sexy cute

SSDD-	Same *stuff* different day
SSEWBA-	Someday soon, everything will be acronyms
SSIA-	Subject says it all
SSIF-	So stupid it's funny
SSINF-	So stupid it's not funny
STBX-	Soon to be ex
STBY-	Sucks to be you
ST&D-	Stop texting and drive
STD-	Seal the deal / Sexually transmitted disease
STFU-	Shut the *freak* up
STFW-	Search the *freaking* web
STH-	something
STM-	Spank the monkey/ spend the money
STPPYNOZGTW-	Stop picking your nose, get to work
STR8-	Straight
STS-	So to speak
STW-	Search the web
STYS-	Speak to you soon
SU-	Shut up
SUAC-	*Stuff* up a creek
SUAKM-	Shut up and kiss me
SUFI-	Super finger / shut up *freaking* imbecile
SUFID-	Screwing up face in disgust
SUITM-	See you in the morning
SUL-	Snooze you lose/ see you later
SUP-	What's up?
SUX-	Sucks
SUYF-	Shut up you fool
SWAG-	Scientific wild *butt* guess / software & giveaways
SWAK-	Sealed (or sent) with a kiss
SWALBCAKWS-	Sealed with a lick because a kiss won't stick

SWALK-	Sealed with a loving kiss
SWAT-	Scientific wild *booty* guess
SWDYT-	So what do you think?
SWEET<3-	Sweetheart
SWF-	Single white female
SWIM-	See what I mean?
SWIS-	See what I'm saying
SWL-	Screaming with laughter
SWM-	Single white male
SWMBO-	She who must be obeyed
SWU-	So what's up?
SYL-	See you later
SYR-	Slow your role
SYS-	See you soon
SYT-	See you tomorrow
S^-	What's up?

-T-

T+-	Think positive
T4BU-	Thanks for being you
T:)T-	Think happy thoughts
T&C-	Terms & conditions
T@YL-	Talk at you later
TA-	Thanks again/thanks a lot
TABOOMA-	Take a bite out of my *booty*
TAF-	That's all, folks
TAFN-	That's all for now
TAH-	Take a hike
TAKS-	That's a knee slapper
TANJ-	There ain't no justice
TANK-	Really strong
TANKED-	Owned
TANKING-	Owning
TANSTAAFL-	There ain't no such thing as a free lunch
TAP-	Take a pill
TARFU-	Things are really *fouled* up
TAS-	Taking a shower
TAU-	Thinking about you (u)
TAUMUALU-	Thinking about you miss you always love you
TAW-	Teachers are watching
TBA-	To be advised/ to be announced
TBAG-	Process of disgracing a corpse/ taunting a flagged/killed player (online gaming)
TBC-	To be continued
TBD-	To be determined
TBE-	Thick between ears

TBH-	To be honest
TBT-	To be truthful/ to be true
TBYB-	Try before you buy
TC-	Take care
TCB-	Trouble came back/ take(ing) care of business
TCOY-	Take care of yourself
TDM-	Too darn many
TDTM-	Talk dirty to me
TEHO-	To each his own
TEOTWAWKI-	The end of the world as we know it
TFDS-	That's for darn sure
TFH-	Thread from Hades
TFLMS-	Thanks for letting me share
TFM-	Thanks from me
TFMIU-	The *freaking* manual is unreadable
TFN-	Thanks for nothing /til further notice
TFS-	Thanks for sharing /three finger salute
TFTHAOT-	Thanks for the help ahead of time
TFTT-	Thanks for the thought
TFX-	Traffic
TGAL-	Think globally, act locally
TGBTG-	To God be the glory
TGGTG-	that girl/guy has got to go
TGIF-	Thank God it's Friday
THX /TX/ THKS-	Thanks
THT-	Think happy thoughts
THNX-	Thanks
THNQ-	Thank you
TIA-	Thanks in advance
TIAD-	Tomorrow is another day
TIAIL-	Think I am in love
TIC-	Tongue in cheek

TIE-	Take it easy
TIEZ-	Take it easy/ taking it easy
TIGAS-	Think I give a *crap*
TILII-	Tell it like it is
TILIS-	Tell it like it is
TINGTES-	There is no gravity, the earth sucks
TINWIS-	That is not what I said
TISC-	This is so cool
TISL-	This is so lame
TISNC-	This is so not cool
TISNF-	That is so not fair
TISNT-	That is so not true
TK-	To come
TKU4UK-	Thank you for your kindness
TLA-	Three letter acronym
TLC-	Tender loving care
TLGO-	The list goes on
TLITBC-	That's life in the big city
TLK2UL8R-	Talk to you later
TM-	Trust me
TMA-	Too many acronyms
TMB-	Text me back
TMI-	Too much information
TMSGO-	Too much *stuff* going on
TMTOWTDI-	There's more than one way to do it
TMOT-	Trust me on this
TMWFI-	Take my word for it
TNA-	Temporarily not available
TNC-	Tongue in cheek
TNSTAAFL-	There's no such thing as a free lunch
TNT-	Til next time
TNTL-	Trying not to laugh

TNX-	Thanks
TOBAL-	There ought a be a law
TOBG-	This ought a be good
TOE-	Terms of endearment
TOGONOOKLEER-	To explode
TOJ-	Tears of joy
TOM-	Tomorrow
TOPCA-	Til our paths cross again
TOS-	Terms of service
TOT-	Tons of time
TOU-	Thinking of you
TOY-	Thinking of you
TP-	Team player / teleport/ totally possible
TPC-	The phone company/the people's choice
TPM-	Tomorrow afternoon (PM)
TPS-	That's pretty stupid
TPT-	Trailer park trash
TPTB-	The powers that be
TQ-	Te quiero (I want you in Spanish)
TQM-	Total quality management
TRAM-	The rest are mine
TRDMC-	Tears running down my cheeks
TRIPDUB-	Triple w (www)
TROO-	True
TRP-	Television rating points
TS-	Tough *stuff* / totally stinks
TSIA-	This Says It All
TSIF-	Thank science it's Friday
TSNF-	That's so not fair
TSOB-	Tough son of a *biscuit*
TSR-	Totally stuck in ram / totally stupid rules
TSRA-	Two shakes of a rat's *butt*

TSTB-	The sooner the better
TT-	Big tease
TTA-	Tap that *butt*
TTBOMK-	To the best of my knowledge
TTFN-	Ta-ta for now
TTG-	Time to go
TTIOT-	The truth is out there
TTKSF-	Trying to keep a straight face
TTLY-	Totally
TTMF-	Ta-ta *MOFO*
TTS-	Text to speech
TTT-	That's the ticket / to the top / thought that too
TTTH-	Talk to the hand
TTTHTFAL-	Talk to the hand the face ain't listening
TTTKA-	Time to totally kick ass
TTTT-	To tell the truth
TTUL-	Talk to you later
TTYAWFN-	Talk to you a while from now
TTYL-	Talk to you later / type to you later
TTYS-	Talk to you soon
TTYT-	Talk to you tomorrow
TVM4YEM-	Thank you very much for your e-mail
TWHAB-	This won't hurt a bit
TWHE-	The walls have ears
TWIMC-	To whom it may concern
TWITA-	That's what i'm talking about
TWIWI-	That was interesting, wasn't it?
TWSS-	That's what she said
TXS-	Thanks
TXT IM-	Text instant message
TXT MSG-	Text message
TY-	Thank you

TYAFY-	Thank you and *freak* you
TYCLO-	Turn your **CAPS LOCK** off
TYFC-	Thank you for charity (online gaming/
	Thank you for caring/thank you for coming
TYFYC-	Thank you for your comment
TYG-	There you go
TYS-	Told you so
TYSO-	Thank you so much
TYVM-	Thank you very much

-U-

^URS-	Up yours
U-	You
U UP-	Are you up?
U-L-	You will
U2-	You too
U8-	You ate?
UAD-	Under- age drinking
UBL2M-	You belong to me
UBS-	Unique buying state
UCMU-	You crack me up
UCWAP-	Up a creek without a paddle
UDH82BME-	You'd hate to be me
UDI-	Unidentified drinking injury (bruise)
UDM-	You're the man/ u da man
UDS-	Ugly domestic scene/situation
UFB-	Un *freaking* believable
UFN-	Until further notice
UG2BK-	You've got to be kidding
UGC-	User-generated content
UKTR-	You know that's right
UL-	Upload
U-L-	You will
UNA-	Use no acronyms
UN4GTBLE-	Unforgettable
UN4TUN8-	Unfortunate
UNBLEFBLE-	Unbelievable
UNCRTN-	Uncertain
UNPC-	Un-politically correct

UNTCO-	You need to chill out
UOK-	Are you ok?/ you ok?
UPOD-	Under promise over deliver
UR-	You are/your
UR2K-	You are too kind
URAPITA-	You are a pain in the *booty*
URA*-	You are a star
URGR*-	You are great
URH-	You are hot (U R hot)
URSAI-	You are such an idiot
URSKTM-	You are so kind to me
URSK2-	You are so kind too
URTM-	You are the man
URW-	You are welcome
URWS-	You are wise
URYY4M-	You are too wise for me
URZ-	Yours
USP-	Unique selling proposition
USU-	Usually
UT-	Unreal tournament (online gaming)
UT2L-	You take too long
UTM-	You tell me
UV-	Unpleasant visual/ ultra violet
UW-	Your welcome
UWIWU-	You wish I was you
UYWIM-	You know what I mean

V-	Victory
VBG-	Very big grin
VBS-	Very big smile
VC-	Venture capital
VCDA-	Vaya con dios, amigo (Goodbye, go with God, Friend)
VEG-	Very evil grin
VFF-	Very *freaking* funny
VFM-	Value for money
VGC-	Very good condition
VGH-	Very good hand (online gaming)
VGN-	Vegan / vegetarian
VHF-	Very happy face
VIP-	Very important person
VIV-	Very important visitor
VM-	Voice mail
VN-	Very nice
VNH-	Very nice hand (online gaming)
VRBS-	Virtual reality bull *stuff*
VRY-	Very
VSC-	Very soft chuckle
VSF-	Very sad face
VWD-	Very well done
VWP-	Very well played

W@-	What
W'S^-	What's up?
W/-	With
W/B-	Welcome back
W/E-	Weekend
W/O-	Without
W/R/T-	With regard to
W00T-	We own the other team
W3-	WWW (web address)
W4M-	Women for men
W8-	Wait
W9-	Wife in room
WAD-	Without a doubt
WAEF-	When all else fails
WAFB-	What a *freaking* *biscuit*
WAFM-	What a *freaking mess
WAFS-	Warm and fuzzies
WAFWHIJ-	What a friend we have in Jesus
WAG-	Wild *butt* guess
WAH-	Work at home
WAI-	What an idiot
WAJ-	What a jerk
WAK-	What a kiss
WAM-	Wait a minute
WAMBAM-	Web application meets brick and mortar
WAMH-	With all my heart
WAMM-	With all my might
WAN2-	Want to?

WAN2TLK-	Want to talk
WAREZ-	Pirated (illegally gained) software
WAS-	Wait a second
WAWA-	Where are we at?
WAYD-	What are you doing?
WAYF-	Where are you from?
WAYN-	Where are you now?
W/B-	Write back
WB-	Welcome back / write back
WBS-	Write back soon
WBU-	What 'bout you?
WC-	Who cares?/ welcome
WCA-	Who cares anyway?
WD-	Well done
WDALYIC-	Who died and left you in charge?
WDDD-	Whoopee doo da dey
WDYK-	What do you know
WDR-	With due respect
WDT-	Who does that?
WDYM-	What do you mean?
WDYMBT-	What do you mean by that?
WDYS-	What did you say?
WDYT-	What Do You Think?
W/E-	Weekend
WE-	Whatever
W/END-	Weekend
WEG-	Wicked evil grin
WEP-	Weapon
WEIG-	With everything I got
WETSU-	We eat this *stuff* up
WF-	Way fun
WFM-	Works for me

WG-	Wicked grin
WGAFF-	Who gives a flying *freak*
WGUMCD-	What goes up must come down
WH5-	Who, what, when, where, why
WIBAMU-	Well, I'll be a monkey's uncle
WIBNI-	Wouldn't it be nice if
WID-	When in doubt...
WIIFM-	What's in it for me?
WIIFY-	What's in it for you?
WILB-	Workplace internet leisure browsing
WILCO-	Will comply
WIM-	Woe is me
WIP-	Work in progress
WIRLD-	World
WISP-	Winning is so pleasurable
WIT-	Wordsmith in training
WITFITS-	What in the *freak* is this *stuff*
WITP-	What is the point?
WITW-	What in the world
WIU-	Wrap it up
WK-	Week
WKD-	Weekend
WKEWL-	Way cool
WL-	What a loser/ with love
WLMIRL-	Would like to meet in real life
WMHGB-	Where many have gone before
WMMOWS-	Wash my mouth out with soap
WMPL-	Wet my pants laughing
WNOHGB-	Where no one has gone before
W/O-	Without
WOA-	Work of art
WOG-	Wise old guy

WOM-	Word of mouth
WOMBAT-	Waste of money, brains and time
WOOF-	Well off older folks
WOOT-	We own the other team
WOP-	Without papers
WORD-	It means cool, a.k.a. word up
WOTAM-	Waste of time and money
WOTD-	Word of the day
WP-	Well Played
WRK-	Work
WRT-	With regard to /with respect to
WRU-	Where are you?
WRU@-	Where are you at?
WRUD-	What are you doing?
WRUDATM-	What are you doing at the moment?
WT-	Without thinking / what the / who the
WTB-	Want to buy
WTF-	What the *freak*
WTFDYJS-	What the *freak* did you just say?
WTFE-	What the *freak* ever
WTFGDA-	Way to *freaking* go, dumb *butt*
WTFH-	What the *freaking* *Hades*
WTFWYCM-	Why the *freak* would you call me?
WTG-	Way to go
WTGP-	Want to go private?
WTH-	What the heck
WTHOW-	White trash headline of the week
WTM-	Who's the man?
WTMI-	Way too much information
WTN-	What then now? / Who then now?
WTS-	Want to sell
WTSDS-	Where the sun don't shine

WTSHTF-	When the *stuff* hits the fan
WTTM-	Without thinking too much
WU-	What's up?
WUCIWUG-	What you see is what you get
WUF-	Where you from
WUP-	What up?
WUU2-	What you up to?
WUW-	What you (u) want
WUWH-	Wish you were here
WUWHIMA-	Wish you were here in my arms
WUZ-	Was
WUZ4DINA-	What's for dinner?
WUZUP-	what's up?
WWJD-	What would Jesus do?
WWNC-	Will wonder never cease
WWSD-	What would Satan do?
WWY-	Where were you?
WWYC-	Write when you can
WX-	Weather
WYCM-	Will you call me?
WYD-	What you doing?
WYFM-	Would you *freak* me?
WYGAM-	When you get a minute
WYGISWYPF-	What you get is what you pay for
WYHAM-	When you have a minute
WYLEI-	When you least expect it
WYM-	What do you mean?
WYMYN-	Women
WYP-	What's your problem?
WYRN-	What's your real name?
WYS-	Whatever you say
WYSILOB-	What you see is a load of bullocks

WYSIWYG-	What you see is what you get
WYSLPG-	What you see looks pretty good
WYT-	Whatever you think
WYWH-	Wish you were here

:X:

X-I-10-	Exciting
X-	Kiss
X!-	Meaning a typical woman
XD-	Really hard/ devilish smile
XL-	Excel/ extra large
XXL-	Extra extra large
XLNT-	Excellent
XLR8-	Accelerate (go faster)
XME-	Excuse me
XOXO-	Hugs and kisses
XQZT-	Exquisite
XTC-	Ecstasy
XYL-	Ex-young lady (wife)/amateur radio
XYZ-	Examine your zipper

- Y -

Y? -	Why?
Y-	Why? / yes
Y2K-	You're too kind
YA-	Yet another
YA -YAYA-	Yet another ya-ya (as in yo-yo)
YAA-	Yet another acronym
YABA-	Yet another bloody acronym
YACC-	Yet another calendar company
YAFIYGI-	You asked for it you got it
YAJWD-	You ain't just whistling Dixie
YAOTM-	Yet another off topic message
YARLY-	Yeah really
YAUN-	Yet another UNIX nerd
YBF-	You've been *freaked*
YBIC-	Your brother in Christ
YBS-	You'll be sorry
YBY-	Yeah baby yeah
YBYSA-	You bet your sweet *butt*
YCDBWYCID-	You can't do business when your computer is down
YCHT-	You can have them
YCLIU-	You can look it up
YCMU-	You crack me up
YCT-	Your comment to
YDKM-	You don't know me
YEPPIES-	Young experimenting perfection seekers
YF-	Wife
YFF-	Young fresh and fly

YGBK-	You gotta be kidding
YGBSM-	You gotta be *crapping* me
YG-	Young gentleman
YGG-	You go girl
YGLT-	You're gonna love this
YGM-	You've got mail
YGTBK-	You've got to be kidding
YGTBKM-	You've got to be kidding me
YGWYPF-	You get what you pay for
YHBT-	You have been tricked/trolled
YHBW-	You have been warned
YHL-	You have lost
YHM-	You have mail
YIC-	Yours in Christ
YIU-	Yes, I understand
YIWGP-	Yes, I will go private
YKW-	You know what?
YKWIM-	You know what I mean
YKWYCD-	You know what you can do
YL-	Young lady
YM-	Your mother
YMAK-	You may already know
YMMV-	Your mileage may vary
YNK-	You never know
YOYO-	You're on your own
YR-	Yeah right/ your
YRYOCC-	You're running on your own coo-coo clock
YS-	You stinker
YSAN-	You're such a nerd
YSDIW8-	Why should I wait?
YSIC-	Why should I care?/ Your sister in Christ
YSK-	You should know

YSYD-	Yeah, sure you do
YT-	You there?
YTB-	You're the best
YTG-	You're the greatest
YTRNW-	Yeah that's right, now what?
YTTL-	You take too long
YTTT-	You telling the truth?
YUPPIES-	Young urban professionals
YW-	You're welcome
YWIA-	You're welcome in advance
YWHNB-	Yes, we have no bananas
YWSYLS-	You win some you lose some
YY4U-	Too wise for you
YYSSW-	Yeah, yeah, sure, sure, whatever

- Z -

Z-	Zero/said
Z's-	Meaning going to sleep/bed
Z%-	Zoo
ZERG-	To gang up on someone
ZH-	Sleeping hour
ZMG -	Oh my God/ oh my gosh
ZOMG-	Used in World of War craft (Oh my God)
ZOT-	Zero tolerance
ZUP-	What's up?
ZZZ-	Sleeping/ bored/ tired

Always be considerate of others, because Texting while driving can be

DEADLY!

CPSIA information can be obtained at www.ICGtesting.com
Printed in the USA
LVOW011640181211

259993LV00007B/150/P